Mikko Harvey & Jake ~~~~~

IDAHO FALLS

SurVision Books

First published in 2019 by
SurVision Books
Dublin, Ireland
www.survisionmagazine.com

Cover art by Jake Bauer
Cover design by Aviva Malz

ISBN: 978-1-912963-02-7

CONTENTS

Fun

I'm pulling the quills off a dead porcupine
with my toes. Who knows
if my brother will forgive me
ever – ever for just handing him over to the mortuary.
In this life we punch each other in the kidneys.
In the next we lick each other to pieces.
In between, the meat is so rare
it hums in the mouth like glossolalia.

Idaho Falls

Everyone in the office used to be friends. Gregg,
my therapist, used to say *I spy...* before pummeling me
with some juicy wisdom... *a trembling Timmy
afraid of his hands again,* etc.
                                          He was right.
My hands are like nudity: most of the time,
everything you thought you wanted to see
turns out grey, misshapen, holding a gun to your head.

The marina used to be a good place to score.

Time has a funny way of looking like an ice cube, huh?
Deirdre used to pluck my back hairs
with such big tweezers I called them
jaws of life. She hated me.

Please, stop singing about money. Everyone
in the office used to be friends. Everyone in the office
used to have funny, ice cube hands,

and the worst custard in the world used to be made
in Idaho Falls, Idaho, where Jim and I
got so high we almost understood each other,
standing naked in separate dressing rooms in Macy's.

Double-Blind

Ladies and gentlemen —
    for breakfast she ate two human babies with hot sauce,
the man in the top hat bragged, jabbing an electric stick
into the flank of the enormous, tranquilized beast, which
sterilized me a bit, I admitted, but Tracy said *Set your jets off,*
Ivan. You wanted this, remember? It was true, I had asked her
to teach me the difference between death and the scientific
method, and it was true, she looked reality in the face
while I was always peeking up at it from a foxhole,
and it was true, nobody'd ever loved me as much as she did,
but in that moment, witnessing Death for the first time,
all I could do was eat my jujubes. I wanted to duck down
under the whiz of crossfire and lob a grenade at it.
I wanted to lead the beast by the hand out of the arena.
Tracy wanted me to be able to do the dishes without crying.
The beast wanted to crash through the forests of Brazil
like the Cerberus in the tattoo Tracy has in bronze
across her chest. *Relax, folks: the babies were already dead.*

Walking home in the rain, I felt like a careful bird.
Sometimes the beauty of this world ruins me.

A Tale of Friendship

Hula hooping is hard because
I live on a submarine, where Dad shoots missiles
and Mom died 1,167 days ago
and Bill from school needs room –
he needs a lot of room to be himself.
Bill also cries a lot.
I have personally witnessed every person
on this submarine cry at least once. Also every single person
has forgotten god.
I am scared of the ugly
red light.
Mom's final word was *what,*
and I guess I knew what she meant:
hula hooping is hard because

Moscow, Pennsylvania

The first best thing

was that past the field of neon butterflies was this
plain tree stump where you could sit and feel nothing

but the crisp mouth of living in a world without magic
tickling the wet matchbook where your brain-brain

was once a problem for the Master of Ceremonies,
but now he simply regards as one more sculpture

in the garden, one more fallen butterfly, its wings
suddenly turned into ziplock baggies full of ideas.

The second best thing was when the Master cleaned
your ears.

to the understory – *The*
world is a series of balloons
popping, a chain reaction
that connects appearances
to their nothingness. Ever
since, I figured I'd call
the ground, *book;*
the night, *glove.*
When my daughter steps
in and tells me I'm a failure,
I look at her for a long time.
Then say *Feather, honey.*
Don't you mean feather?

RSVP ASAP

I invited the goat in for a tea party. I invited the fox
to get off my fucking property immediately.
I invited some milk down my throat. It felt strange
inviting all my mortal enemies into my home,
but my noble steed said it had to be done, which it did.
Heron invited bluegill who invited the newborn elk.
Funny how these shitbags come out of the woodwork.
Can everybody hear me? I have an announcement.
My enemies turned to face me, so trusting.
There's raspberry or lemon-ginger iced tea on the counter.
I know it's hot as heck out there. So drink up and then—
Hey, hey, hey, no fucking smoking in here, Parrot!
A little respect, okay?—then we'll play some games.
How about a little cut-your-throat music, I thought,
firing up my modern Scottish folk playlist.
Quacker and Hoot-Hoot were up first for Twister.
I could tell by their footwork they were already
feeling it. A fight broke out at the Uno table
because the rabbits couldn't see straight.
Pin the Tail on the Donkey went as you'd guess:
nightmarish dismemberment. Blood spilled.
The fun was really more than a barrel
of monkeys. It was nine monkeys coming to terms
with the poison, vomiting out the window
till Mom got home from work. By then,
half the guests were dead and the other half

would soon be on fire. *Clean up your toys, Elise.*
K Mom, I said, and thought of the fox. I hoped by now
she was in Canada. I hoped she was strong.
Probably a fox like that is worth a thousand moms.

Prayer

Fondly, I
flipped my juiciest
beetle toward the
wet and flailing
Master of Ceremonies –
even his all-knowingness
unable to sidestep
that which, he had
once forewarned,
would be like a
horse's whinny
ringing in your
ear so quiet it
could fit on a
fingertip if
only it had
a body, which,
of course, it
did now and –

       Sister, you said, *I have a gift for you,*
plunging a beetle into my mouth, past my tonsils.
I swallowed it; its legs tickled my throat, memory-like.
And I saw myself through every drowned pair of eyes.
I saw myself: bubblegum, beetle, fish, church, beetle,
and heard myself on the shore say *I am the queen of grey
childhoods.*

Walking the Bird Dog

Pardon me, dear neighbor, but I noticed—
just now—I've always wanted you more
than I wanted myself.

Lecture

Sitting under the only tree
planted on the roof of the skyscraper,

we watched, with binoculars,

a man across the street
cut off his pinky with a pair of scissors.

Carla looked at me. I looked back at her.

I forget which one of us
laughed first.

That's how good television was, then.

Current Island

The tent appeared to be
overflowing with the kind
of emptiness only bad
intentions trick you into seeing.
Not that Petra isn't the love of my life,
or that Gus doesn't know his way
around a hammer, or that I'm not
a 15-year-old boy pretending
I'm not terrified of being trusted –
nonetheless: where was the lizard?
Am I not the silkiest
caterpillar on the island?
The lies I've told myself
are beginning to lie to each other.
We'd been sent here to discover
friendship. Instead, we named the lizard
Friendship and worshipped it
as we used to worship
Dev, on the
other island. Not
that the current island
isn't the love of my life,
or that the current island doesn't
know its way around a hammer…

Man in the Painting

This painting has the word Brad on it.
My name is Brad.
The woman in the painting is not
my wife. My wife
is a fletcher and
she's not drowning, I hope. She's good
at swimming as well as fletching, and she would never
use a phone underwater, but she did call me
an easily tricked man once. So
much for having too much
of love never being a bad thing. The woman
is in love with the man with a sheet on his head,
presumably. The sheet
was taken from the bed of the ballerina.
I'm no expert, but it seems to me
that people always want less
the water itself and more the soaked skin.
Okay, I admit: I didn't
come to the museum because I like art.
Ever heard the one about the guy
who married a pelican?
That's me, Brad. *The* Brad. If you can't
be the star of your own joke (I was
lying earlier about the fletcher stuff,
and the having-a-wife-at-all stuff –
the thought of you knowing

who I really am,
like a spider, tickles me badly)
then you might as well be a Flemish landscape painting
trapped in the warehouse as it burns down.

Brad's Wife

Maybe I shouldn't eat jujubes for breakfast, she said.
Maybe I shouldn't be so friendly with the Ruler, she said.
But she wants what she wants, and everything else
is just the possum she ran over in her chariot yesterday.
Poor possum – it probably had a great personality.

The Part the Newspaper People Talk About

Being from around here is like picking apples
then using them to break the windows
of your ex-boyfriend's dad's new Porsche in his driveway.
That's the part the newspaper people don't talk about.
Sometimes boys like Spencer don't get pushed
off bridges, sometimes they do. Sometimes
girls like Molly get pregnant without ever having sex.
So when the old army-faced cheetah-hunter turned
up in town, no one really paid him much mind.
But I did get curious a few days later
when I found him sharpening his knife and muttering
what goes around and around and around…
until he flung it into the pond and I couldn't
tell what his tears meant. Stella calls them
stumblebums. And around here sometimes parents
like mine hurt each other for fun. But this stumblebum
wasn't about to teach me how to shoot
a crossbow just "for fun." This was about standing up
in the middle of a thicket, looking that
cheetah-critter straight in the eye until we understood
its very critterness, then…
Things that happen are supposed to happen. Colin
says gravity means we're just always stuck here.

Cartwheeler

The miracle
wagon rumbles
in carrying
a single

adolescent fox.
I'm available
to try some

fox meat, I volunteer,
calling out from
the window

of the church's
basement, which is
where they keep me.

When the town's all
busy with its Loyalty
Festival, the basement

grows shadowless,
my bread finally
sad and relaxed.

There's a ditty
in the bureau
I wear like a belt –

but that bureau
is closed forever.
The King murdered

a schoolboy, murmurs
the bread while I
practice cartwheels.

If regular, then
you may as well
relieve your grace

of its wings.
I quiver
when its misty;
I romance the ceiling.

Annual Games

I.

Although every neck is crooked upward to see
the hot air balloon battle, Hank's neck is especially
giraffed up over the armory of leaves, making him
my favorite.

II.

*Have you seen the humorous new film about
circumcision?* the woman beside me at the grenade toss
remarked to her friend, who began laughing
uncontrollably.

III.

　*Ma looks pretty much as pretty
as she always did,* you said, as

the party was ending as

our time here was ending as

the sky sizzled as

you touched my ear as

We Usually Never Spoke of California Since the War

Shiv loved Magellan too much. She cooked sausage
too often. She was always questioning me. I don't know
anything about Great Gatsby! Plus it didn't help
that she smelled kind of like godmom did. Every day
in August we ran into each other, due to her having
built a makeshift cabana beside the condo's jacuzzi,
where she pretty much lived. *Listen, cowboy*, Remi said,
she's right as rain and smart as rain and kind as rain.
She just misses California. California.

Hell, we all missed California. I remember
when Remi and I shared the job of college mascot:
he was the cloud and I was the thunderbolt.
She calls herself Shiv because she once gutted
the mayor and took his supplies; there were several ways
to outlast the mermaids. Chex Mix and rats worked
for me. Blood-stained mer-scales caught the sun prettily,
prettily – like a fast horse or stained glass in Iowa
City, where we first began to believe the absence
of god was the presence of light. I've heard of raindrops
so heavy that when they hit a rat in the head, it never
sleeps again. Never ever ever sleeps again.

Archibald, Could You Hand Me My Soul Please

from the cheese drawer?
I got a lotta bizness
in town today regarding
your suicide. Gotta line

fourteen crumpled
apologies up in a row (like you
used to say, you used to say)
"sexually," "morally,"

"scientifically"
on the porch swing. I think things
should be allowed to be
what they are,

only. Remember,
you tossed a Frisbee
straight through the fog
of me? I misted it.

Life makes a joke
out of the joke we were trying
to make life-like. Every scientist
contains a tiny babushka

knitting tinier blindfolds.
And when I sit motionless
in my gazebo at dawn…
shit. Sometimes I think

I really fucked up.

Compendium of the Mailwoman

The mailwoman liked playing a game
where she scribbled W. Benjamin quotes on the envelopes
she was paid to deliver to children she respected.

*

Once when she was a child, the mailwoman painted
her father's sleeping body green, like after grass
is mown and piles up, pathetically.

*

Before she was a mailwoman, the mailwoman
stormed castles in Europe on her horse named Cusco.
The castles were always empty.

*

The mailwoman had a thought—
the world is already dead, so you cannot harm it—
which she tucked under her armpit.

*

The mailwoman refused to say her real name in a world
where unidentified flying objects were real
and owls, in the end, were proven a hoax.

*

Acting on a hunch, the mailwoman ran
several blocks, entered the forest, climbed the fifteenth maple
she saw, and died up there.

*

At the community meeting the community agreed
that they were a community. Afterwards,
the mailwoman arrived with a package for Stan.

*

The mailwoman is an idea.
There are no known photographs of Cusco.

*

The mailwoman was not (as some of her friends said)
"unfairly cruel to those who whistled in public."
She did chastise them, however, like any rational,
intelligent, kind, law-abiding, conscientious citizen would.

*

The mailwoman had a penchant for pendants, pretending
one pendant was the parent of another pendant
and parents weren't painful memories.

*

The mailwoman once described her relationship
with dada as somewhere
helicopters cannot land.

*

The mailwoman schlepped in a hand-woven basket
a magnifying glass, raw carrots, three girl dolls,
a stone from Belize, Brecht's *Selected*, and aerosol cheese.

*

The mailwoman sometimes examined
the vomit the youth left behind on the steps, sifting
for answers.

*

The mailwoman smashed a window because it was perfect.

Prayer

I managed to haggle the vender down from 27
strands of brown hair—he knew well as anyone
brown hair was scarce at the Bazaar of Lice—
to 60 blond ones. Haggling is all about
shame tactics, which is why Papa taught me
this dance. The movements are imperceptible
shmimperheptible; you either got it
or you don't. Then I took my new louse to Papa.
He was dying. He wanted one more for his circus.

*

The neighborhood really snuggled around gossip.
The mailwoman believed gossip was worse than murder
(the cosmic shudder induced by the experience of the invisible).

*

And the catalogues! And the catalogues! In the 80s,
the mailwoman catalogued the hollows squirrels drank frc
while everyone else was getting high with their friends.

More poetry published by SurVision Books

Noelle Kocot. *Humanity*
(New Poetics: USA)
ISBN 978-1-9995903-0-7

Ciaran O'Driscoll. *The Speaking Trees*
(New Poetics: Ireland)
ISBN 978-1-9995903-1-4

Elin O'Hara Slavick. *Cameramouth*
(New Poetics: USA)
ISBN 978-1-9995903-4-5

Anatoly Kudryavitsky. *Stowaway*
(New Poetics: Ireland)
ISBN 978-1-9995903-2-1

George Kalamaras. *That Moment of Wept*
ISBN 978-1-9995903-7-6

Christopher Prewitt. *Paradise Hammer*
(Winner of James Tate Poetry Prize 2018)
ISBN 978-1-9995903-9-0

Anton Yakovlev. *Chronos Dines Alone*
(Winner of James Tate Poetry Prize 2018)
ISBN 978-1-912963-01-0

Bob Lucky. *Conversation Starters in the Language No One Speaks*
(Winner of James Tate Poetry Prize 2018)
ISBN 978-1-912963-00-3

Maria Grazia Calandrone. *Fossils*
Translated from Italian
(New Poetics: Italy)
ISBN 978-1-9995903-6-9

Sergey Biryukov. *Transformations*
Translated from Russian
(New Poetics: Russia)
ISBN 978-1-9995903-5-2

Anton G. Leitner. *Selected Poems 1981–2015*
Translated from German
ISBN 978-1-9995903-8-3

Our books are available to order via
http://survisionmagazine.com/books.htm

*

The neighborhood really snuggled around gossip.
The mailwoman believed gossip was worse than murder
(the cosmic shudder induced by the experience of the invisible).

*

And the catalogues! And the catalogues! In the 80s,
the mailwoman catalogued the hollows squirrels drank from
while everyone else was getting high with their friends.

Prayer

I managed to haggle the vender down from 27
strands of brown hair—he knew well as anyone
brown hair was scarce at the Bazaar of Lice—
to 60 blond ones. Haggling is all about
shame tactics, which is why Papa taught me
this dance. The movements are imperceptible
shmimperheptible; you either got it
or you don't. Then I took my new louse to Papa.
He was dying. He wanted one more for his circus.